Remaking

poems by

KM Kramer

Finishing Line Press
Georgetown, Kentucky

Remaking

Copyright © 2026 by KM Kramer
ISBN 979-8-89990-344-1 First Edition
All rights reserved under International and Pan-American Copyright Conventions. No part of this book may be reproduced in any manner whatsoever without written permission from the publisher, except in the case of brief quotations embodied in critical articles and reviews.

ACKNOWLEDGMENTS

Thank you to the editors of the following journals who published early versions of these poems:

"Full Circle" and "Medusa," *Action Spectacle* (2025)
"I am my own Rapunzel," *Rogue Agent* (2025)
"Shape Series: Cubist Self-Portrait," *Sine Qua Non* (inaugural issue prize finalist)
"The Gift of Betrayal," *Free the Verse* (2025)
"Flaco's Choice," *Last Stanza Poetry Journal* (2025)
"Seagulls and the Sea," *The Prose Poem* (2025) (finalist for 2024 best prose poem)
"Come Back" and "Keeping Busy," *San Antonio Review* (2024)
"The Rose Knows," *RedRoseThorns Magazine* (2024)
"Unmaking Myths," *The Modern Artis*t (2024)

With gratitude, most especially, to Allison Pitinii Davis from Stanford's Continuing Eduction Program. Thank you to Miranda Hope, Mimi Lyons, and Amelia Zimmermann Wolff for your feedback and for making Peninsula Poets happen. To Loren Edelson for believing early on. And to Bob for your supportive presence.

Publisher: Leah Huete de Maines
Editor: Christen Kincaid
Cover Art and Illustrations: Joanna Baker
Author Photo: Herve Philippe
Cover Design: Natalie O'Rourke

Order online: www.finishinglinepress.com
also available on amazon.com

Author inquiries and mail orders:
Finishing Line Press
PO Box 1626
Georgetown, Kentucky 40324
USA

Contents

Unmaking Myths 1

Keeping Busy 2

Shape Series: The Lamp 3

I am my own Rapunzel 4

Wormhole 5

Full Circle 6

Medusa 6

The gift of betrayal 7

What the Rose Knows 8

The Rose 9

Beyond Regret 10

Shape Series: Cubist Self-Portrait 11

Come Back 12

Palo Alto, California 13

Flaco's Choice 14

Shape Series: Playing the Odds 16

Circe's Reversal 17

Seagulls and the Sea 19

Journey 20

Icarus (Revised) 21

Endnotes 23

Unmaking Myths

AI swallows myths we feed it: that's how
it pretends to be human.

Christopher Columbus. Robert E Lee.
Statues now torn down.

Salud to red wine! To live long!
No, that's wrong.

1998: 1 in 10,000 children have autism.
2024: 1 in 36 children have autism.

Strip the myths, like husks off
corn to reach the kernels.

Light looks white—indisputable.
A prism frees the colors.

Broken bottles in the ocean
soften into sea glass.

Don't worry, I tell myself. *I still may have the last word.* The silenced often do.

Keeping Busy

Running through
the bee swarms

not stopping to feel
the stings

but in the stillness
of my dreams

the welts erupt.

Shape Series: The Lamp

Crouched
at the stairwell,

we eavesdrop, hearing
tones, but not the words:

(Her) Scream—hiss—hiss.
(Him) Low hum, swish, swish.

The rhythms alternate:
Her blasts. His feather-sweeps.

We peer down
slats

to the family
room, trying to see

but not be
seen.

We strain to hear—
what next?

The next day, in the family room:
the lamp, its ceramic base of stacked books,

accents the end-table as usual. One has to look close
to see the crack. It zig zags down

the spines. As if nothing happened, the pieces
crazy-glued back together.

I am my own Rapunzel

with the towel knotted and draped
atop my head. Like the ends of tresses,
the terry cloth edges fringe
my waist. I toss

my head of towel-hair—
feel the long locks sweep
past my shoulder, down my back.
The girl looking back in the mirror

looks nothing like the skinny girl,
dark-haired in tufts as sparse as a newly
seeded lawn. Nothing like the girl who wears
a baseball cap each day of second grade

to cover her hoed scalp, to contain
the smell of pus. Before the mirror,
I twist to see if my back looks pink
again with flesh. Instead: yellow-brown

patches of scabs. Hot pink where one
has fallen off. Or where I pick it,
sliding the shower-softened dead flesh
to free the new underneath.

The sink vanity I sit on
cools the back of my thigh. The
mirror fogs, helping me create
the filter of how I look now

three months after the accident.

Wormhole

Full Circle

MEDUSA: Athena, why did you punish me when I needed your help?

ATHENA: I don't know what you're talking about.

MEDUSA: Soon after Neptune raped me in your temple, you found me, weeping, and became angry at me.

ATHENA: I said, I don't know what you are talking about.

MEDUSA: Then why is my hair full of snakes?

ATHENA: I worry about your perception of reality, Medusa.

MEDUSA: OK, look at me.

ATHENA: [*to MEDUSA, aloud*] Why bother? [*as aside*] My heart already is made of stone.

Medusa

The gift of betrayal

—at first, a fisted sandcastle
wreck.
My bare feet settle
on the beach edge
beside the ruins.
The ocean gathers rhythms
to reveal. Rising
with the heat,
the sand smelts
orange
and the grains grind smooth,
cooling into—
(clarity): a looking glass.

What the Rose Knows

You arrive late
but expect to impress,
flourishing a bouquet
of thoughtlessness.
For me?

She's clipped smooth,
her thorns removed.
Stripped from the wild
to be placed
in a porcelain vase.

In hedges:
ordered to
stay in line,
behave.
Tied in twine.

Hallmarked.
Knocked down
on a card.
Flattened.
Glossed over.

But I
have freer and deeper
roots myself.
I root myself
deeper.

The Rose

Beyond Regret

Buried I suffocate
under the hot curdled stink
crushed milk cartons   itchy twigs
half-composted apples
vinegar whiffs two
TVs screens smashed
plastic grocery bags
undigested a sagging
sofa cushion

Somewhere in the Sierras,
an unpaved trail zig zags up
a sun-browned foothill.
Down the other side it branches
into a dozen paths—all flow
into a meadow, infused with lavender.
Oak trees toss picnic blankets
of shade onto the grass,
promising fat acorns.

Shape Series: Cubist Self-Portrait

I am a red
balloon. People point
to me in the sky.
Pumped with helium, I arc
and rock, ready to sail
anywhere

The crow lands its talons on
my temples: *Clench*.
Its beak pokes and gnaws
my eyeholes out. My arms splay
on the cliff rock
(which happens to be my brown couch).
My ankles dangle
down

My chest: the mortar
where the pestle of worry
presses

Stamped. The only
choice: I make the imprint
me. Remade, I am
a lithograph, leaving behind
a series of prints,
increasingly bold

Come Back

Consider
that the groundhog
deserves not to be blamed
because it burrowed for survival
upon winter's arrival.

Spring:
time for him to climb
from his cold, dark hole.
Absence forgiven by the sun.

You, too.

Palo Alto, California

plums sweeten
my backyard

Spanish arches soothe
doorways, corners loosened

3,000 miles from
where my life started

cigarette
smoke is scarce

even the cows look happy
grazing in foothills by the highway

spring: sunshine-painted
passion flowers

Flaco's Choice

*Flaco, the Eurasian eagle-owl at Central Park Zoo
(March 15, 2010 - February 23, 2024)*

Slashing the mesh, vandals gave Flaco a chance
to leave the fake rock, the clipped tree branch and
the painted sky mural—his so-called sanctuary.
Flaco stretched his six-foot wing span.

His flight wobbled at first. People wondered
whether he'd survive among skyscrapers,
telephone wires, and urban forage—
5,000 miles from his native Eurasia.

Police tempted him with a baited cage,
its door open on the sidewalk cement;
muted sirens blinked in red. Sizing it up,
Flaco swiveled his head around

his black & tan argyle chest. He sought
asylum in an elm instead. That night,
100 feet above Central Park, his instincts
for hunt awakened. His eyes glowed gold.

By morning he mastered the catch, belly full.
His flight steadied. His feathers unhunched.
Flaco made Manhattan his own: He perched
on a poet's windowsill, gazing into her world.

He surveyed the sculpture garden on the Lower East
Side. On windy nights he sighed for a mate,
hooting under the stars. He lingered
at cherry and red maple trees—

favoring most the oak at East Drive & 104th.
Fire escape bars became his playground where
he peered at pinched New Yorkers, perhaps
wondering how they felt in their cages.

A year passed. No longer
the "grumpy, slightly pudgy owl"
in Central Park Zoo. One Friday in
February daylight, he careened

into a building on West 89th. He'd ingested
rats infested with poison, the city's gesture for
pest control. Some see a sad ending in his story.
Proof of the vandals' misdeeds. Others

remember mainly this:
In the one year Flaco was free,
he soared—far more than in
all 13 years of captivity.

Shape Series: Playing the Odds

Luck can be a cruel
dealer of cards

I hold four ACES in my hand.
Not the winning four-of-a-
kind, but "Adverse Childhood
Experiences." Physical abuse.
Sexual abuse. Emotional
abuse. Hit by a car.

With four ACES, I face 220%
greater chance of suicide, 80%
increased cancer risk, 100%
higher rate of autoimmune
diseases.

My dear son, autism is no easy
hand for you, either: 85% of
adults who carry this card face
unemployment.

What do we do with these odds?

I say, *Play!*
Play the odds.
Embrace them when

they favor you.
Defy them otherwise: Play
all night; play until you turn

your fate. Laugh at the dealer.
Wink at your friend.
Play until the light

changes to a new
day. Otherwise you
fold

Don't underestimate yourself.
Let the odds be a number, not
the last word.

Circe's Reversal

for Gisèle Pelicot

She slept, drugged.
Bidden by Odysseus,
50 men rolled onto her shore

in turns.
"You have to be clean
without aftershave, no long, dirty

nails," he said. "Cut the sound
if you're not alone." Around 3 a.m.,
he'd signal to his men, "She's free

right now." One responded, "I don't
know how you do this but I dream
of doing the same to my wife

and sharing her with accomplices
like you." Another complained:
"one hour after taking the meds

she is completely asleep.
I don't understand why
we have to wait four hours?"

Unsuspecting Circe thought the problem
was her aging body. You know, pelvic pain,
memory loss—that's menopause for you.

She roughed it for ten years. Then
when Circe caught on to the tricks,
she refused to retreat

to her cave of shame. Instead
she slipped them her own
spell: a flash of light

that cast them as pigs
into the great wide-open
of the Aegean sea.

Pigs that all the world could see
thanks to her courage.
Her witchcraft:

a kind that signaled
we need not be alone
on our own island.

Seagulls and the Sea

From Costa Brava, 60 KM from Salvador Dali's hometown: White ribbons of foam, cinched at the center, flap across the surface of the sea. Seagulls flock; their wings flap, sometimes in a perfect V—in white relief from the cloudless sky. The sky looks connected to the sea. At first, they seem to be mirror images: The blue sky and the blue sea, the white wings beating and the white foam flapping.

The seagulls manage to break free from the frame of sky and sea. Their wings made for resistance, yet able to alight. The untrustworthy sea forces us to notice and forget, with its tide and its undertow.

A conch shell gathers these tricky rhythms into a song. Taking the conch home with me, I play it back from a different seashore. It sounds like a shofar.

Journey

Icarus (Revised)

The true story of Icarus
   differs from the myth—lies, really
     to disguise

what actually happened:
   not a story of failure and hubris;
     a pivot.

The true part: beeswax melted
   his wings' edges while close to the sun.
     But he never fell to the sea.

Minos, so bent
   on control, or its appearance,
     wanted the world to believe

Icarus suffered a terrible fate.
   So Minos paid a ploughman
     by the sea to report a crash.

Yet Icarus flew farther
   than anyone imagined.
     He stopped in the Canary Islands

to rest, assess,
   and repair
     his wings for longer flight.

Let other people have their stories,
   Icarus told himself. He set his sights
     higher: flew to the New World.

All this talk of Icarus today.
   Minos is mostly
     forgotten.

Icarus lives—
 no matter which version
  you choose to believe.

Endnotes

"Playing the Odds"

The incidence of cancer, autoimmune illness and other chronic health problems experienced later in life by children who experience four or more ACES is staggering. Exposure to abuse in childhood, while activating a stress response, also profoundly disrupts the developing nervous system, immune and metabolic systems of children.

For further scientific information about this, see, for example: Bessel Van Der Kolk, M.D., *The Body Keeps Score* (2015); "Vital Signs: Estimated Proportion of Adult Health Problems Attributable to Adverse Childhood Experiences and Implications for Prevention — 25 States, 2015–2017," *CDC Morbidity and Mortality Weekly Report* (Nov. 8 2009); Vincent J Felitti, M.D., "The Relation Between Adverse Childhood Experiences and Adult Health," *Permanente Journal* (2002 Winter). In literature see Stephanie Foo, *What My Bones Know: A Memoir of Healing from Complex Trauma* (Ballantine Books 2022).

"Circe's Reversal"

Gisèle Pelicot discovered her husband repeatedly had drugged her and invited sexual assaults by 50 men nearby over a period of a decade. Defying expectation, at age 72, she allowed the criminal prosecutions of her assailants to take place in open court in France. The quotations consist of real text messages submitted as evidence at trial, which ended in convictions in 2024.

About the artist

Joanna Baker recently graduated from Stanford University where she concentrated on biology and fine arts and completed a capstone in science communication. She grew up in Atlanta, Georgia, and her art has been recognized in competitions such as the Georgia All-State Art Symposium. Joanna created the book cover art as well as all the illustrations.

KM Kramer is a writer, previously a First Amendment attorney, who feels most at home in California. A graduate of Stanford, she received the Letter Review Prize for Poetry and first place in Dreamers Magazine's 2025 Micro Nonfiction Contest. Her work has been published in *Only Poems, MAYDAY Magazine, Action Spectacle, Rogue Agent,* and other journals. Her next collection explores intergenerational trauma. More about her can be found at KMKramerPoetry.com.

www.ingramcontent.com/pod-product-compliance
Lightning Source LLC
Chambersburg PA
CBHW022107080426
42734CB00009B/1506